This book is based on a real trip I took aboard
a barge in Holland. I became fascinated
by the life of barge-people, and my curiosity spurred me on
to learn more about barges and their past.
In addition to the journal of my trip, I have included
drawings of barges from several other countries.
I hope you enjoy this trip, and this book, as much as I did!

First published 1981 by
Librairie Ernest Flammarion, Paris
Original title *Un Voyage en Péniche*
© Flammarion 1981
English language edition © 1982 Huck Scarry
ISBN 0 00 138368 X
First English language edition published 1982
by William Collins Sons & Co Ltd

William Collins Sons & Co Ltd
London · Glasgow · Sydney · Auckland
Toronto · Johannesburg

Travels on a Barge

A Sketchbook by Huck Scarry

Illustrated by the author

In Holland

West Church Tower,
erected in 1631.

Montelbaan Tower,
part of the city fortifications,
built around 1485.

The Mint Tower,
built about 1485.

Recently, I had the opportunity
to take a trip on a barge.
I went to the city of
Amsterdam, in Holland, where
I was to meet the barge
on its journey.
Amsterdam is a lovely city,
crowned by many tall,
slender towers.
I had time to draw some of
the most beautiful ones.

South Church Tower,
built in 1614.

The small "Weepers' Tower,"
where wives bid farewell
to their seafaring husbands.
Built in 1482.

The
"Old Church",
built
in the 1200's.

7

The city of Amsterdam

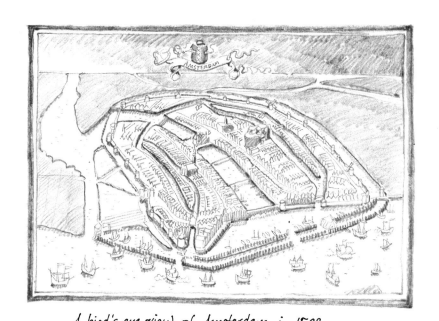

A bird's eye view of Amsterdam in 1538,
drawn from a painting by
Cornelius Antonisz,
now in the Amsterdam Historical Museum.

Most cities
are built along busy avenues,
but the city of Amsterdam
is built around rings
of quiet, graceful canals.
Instead of cars and
trucks, you're likely to
see boats, swans, and ducks
in front of your house.
At a crossroad,
in place of a traffic light
you might find a
beautiful drawbridge.

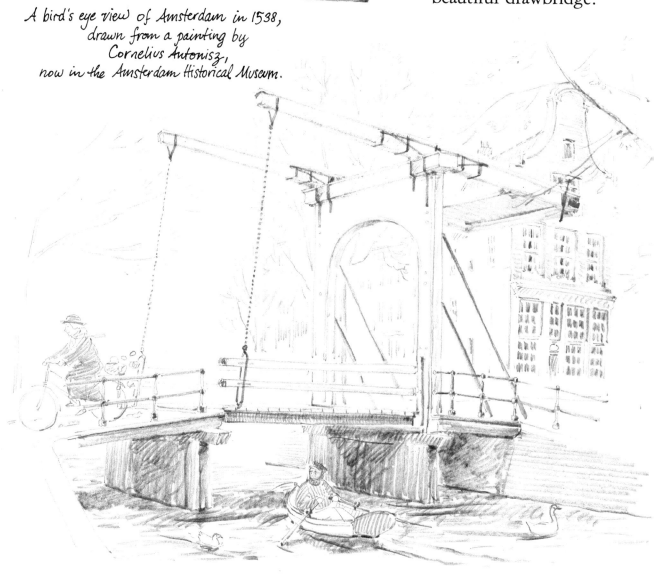

Two of more than 800 bridges which connect the numerous islands of Central Amsterdam.

Every year, about 50 cars take an accidental dip into the canals!

Herengracht.

In winter, when they freeze, the canals make for fine skating.

Amsterdam Harbour

A view of Amsterdam Harbour, drawn from a painting by Willem Van de Velde the Younger, in 1686.

The Royal Palace in the city centre, which was originally built as the Town Hall, in 1655. This impressive edifice gives an idea of Amsterdam's importance already in former times.

With sharp eyes, you'll spot a sailing ship riding proudly above the rooftops!

In the seventeenth century,
Amsterdam was one of the most important ports in the world.
From here, daring captains searched for
a Northwest Passage to the Orient.
From here, the first trading vessels rounded the Cape of Good Hope
on their way to the Far East,
returning with the riches of distant lands.
Today, Amsterdam's harbour is still very busy,
though it is overshadowed by another
Dutch port (Europe's largest),
that of Rotterdam.

When I arrived, the boat I was about to board
was being loaded with sugar beets.
These beets were headed for a sugar refinery
where they'd be processed
to make sugar.

(I have had to shorten the long
ship to fit it onto this page!)

The captain and his wife,
Mr. and Mrs. Van Wynen,
came to meet me
on the dock.
My skipper took my bag,
helped me aboard,
and showed me downstairs
to my cabin.

"As soon as the boat is loaded,
we'll be on our way!"
said the captain.

Much of our sugar comes from sugar beets. Unlike sugar cane, beets can be planted in cool climates, like that of Holland. In 1811, Napoleon ordered that sugar beets be planted all over Europe, after the British had blockaded sugar cane imports to France, from the West Indies.

The shipbuilder's plaque.

Mr. van Wynen's ship is named after another skipper— Mr. van Wynen's father: Adrien Jacopus.

The Adja is a typical, modern Dutch barge:

TONNAGE: 750 Tons	LENGTH: 65 Metres	HORSEPOWER: 500 HP
DRAFT: 2.45 Metres	WIDTH: 7.13 Metres	YEAR BUILT: 1962

13

At home aboard ship

Downstairs,
I had a chance to admire
the Van Wynens'
floating home.
It was spacious
and very neat.
While we waited
for the beets to be
loaded on board,
Mrs. Van Wynen
prepared some coffee,
and the Captain
took a moment to
catch up on . . .

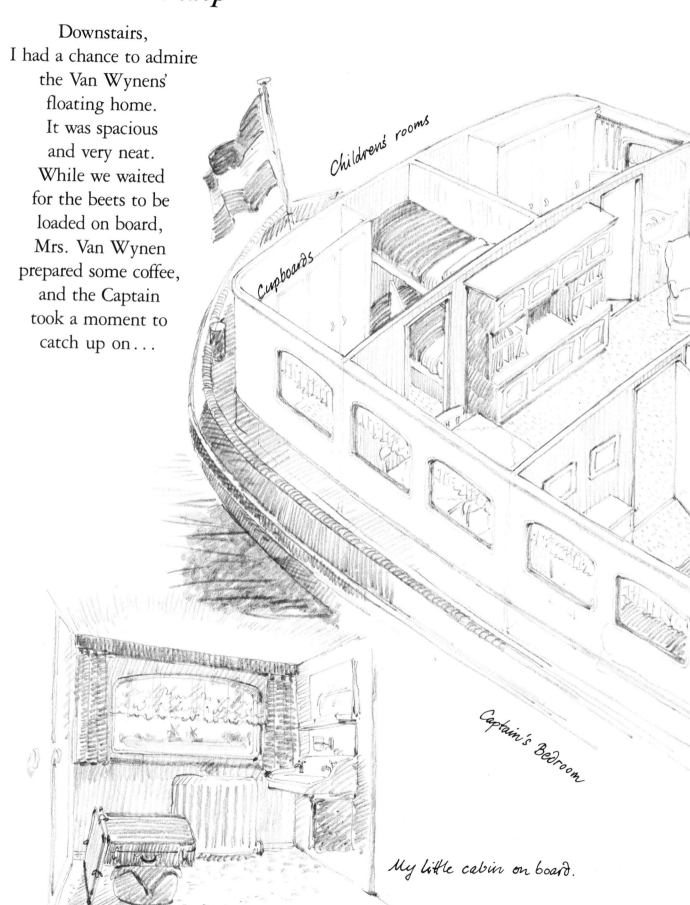

Childrens' rooms

Cupboards

Captain's Bedroom

My little cabin on board.

14

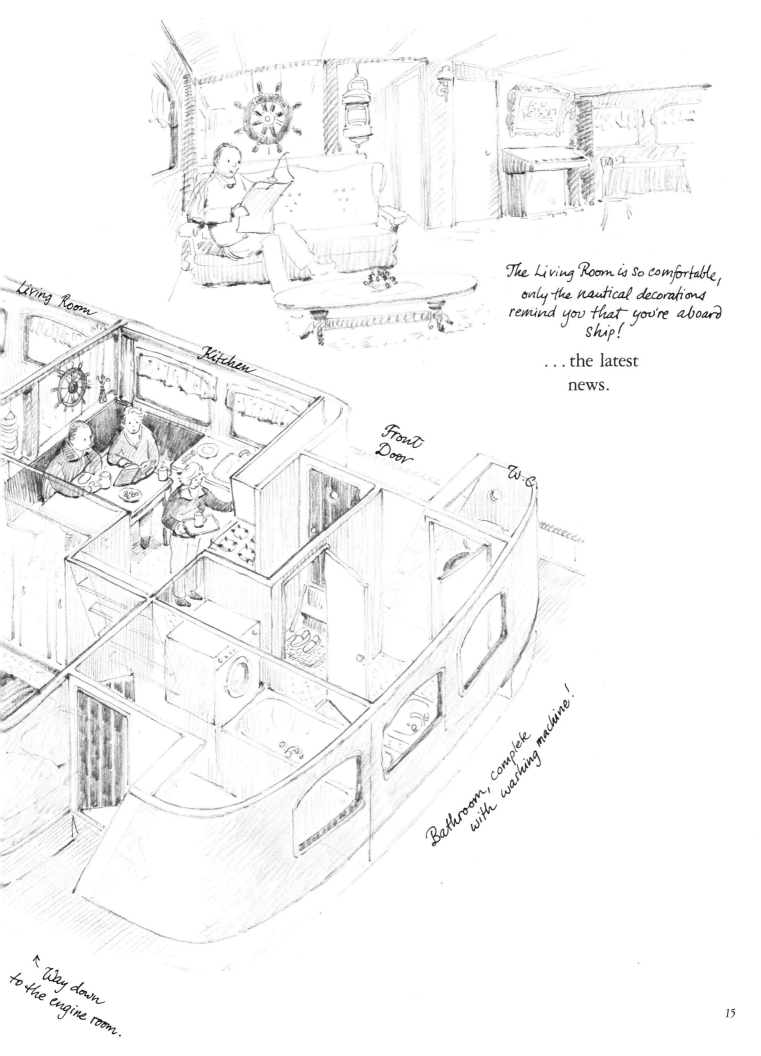

The Living Room is so comfortable, only the nautical decorations remind you that you're aboard ship!

...the latest news.

Living Room

Kitchen

Front Door

W.C.

Bathroom, complete with washing machine!

↑ Way down to the engine room.

In the wheelhouse

By far the most important room
in Captain Van Wynen's house
is the wheelhouse.
From here he guides his barge
along canals as well as rivers.

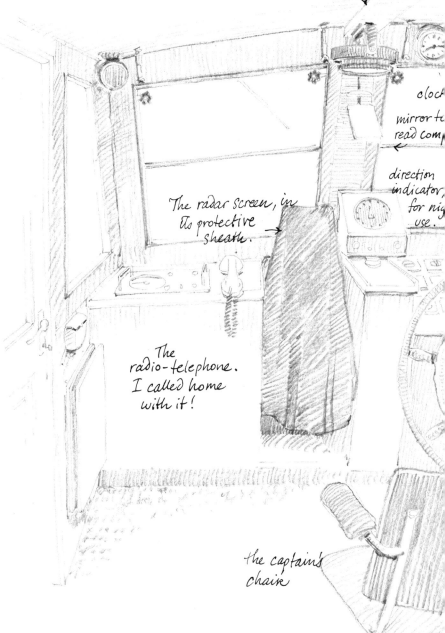

The compass
is placed on the ceiling,
upside-down,
where it is well away
from other metal
instruments.

cloc[k]

mirror t[o]
read com[pass]

direction
indicator,
for nig[ht]
use.

The radar screen, in
its protective
sheath.

The
radio-telephone.
I called home
with it!

the captain's
chair

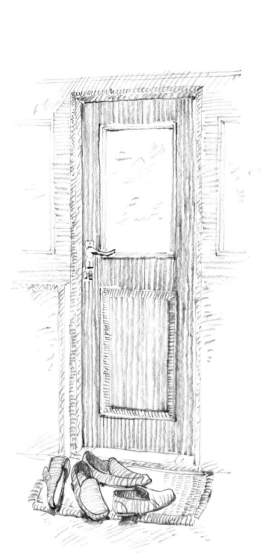

No dirty shoes
allowed in beyond
the doormat!

All the captain's savings go into his barge.
Whenever he can, he buys better and newer equipment,
to keep everything up-to-date.

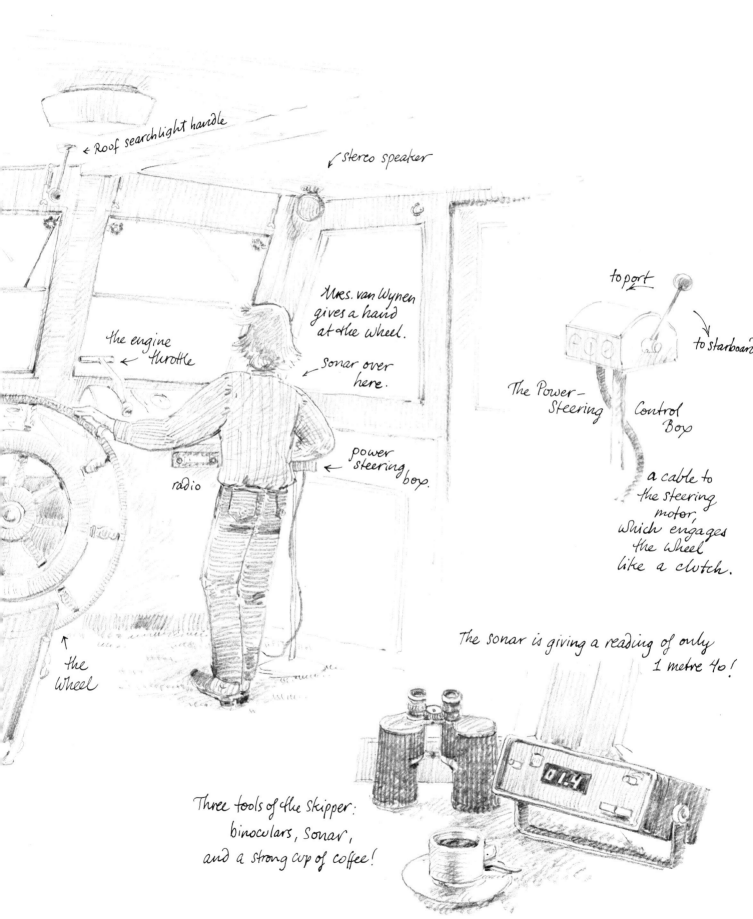

← Roof searchlight handle

↙ stereo speaker

the engine
← throttle

Mrs. van Wynen
gives a hand
at the wheel.

sonar over
here.

to port ←

to starboard ↘

The Power-
Steering   Control
Box

radio

power
steering ←
box.

a cable to
the steering
motor,
which engages
the wheel
like a clutch.

↑
the
Wheel

The sonar is giving a reading of only
1 metre 40!

Three tools of the skipper:
binoculars, sonar,
and a strong cup of coffee!

17

Archimedes' Principle

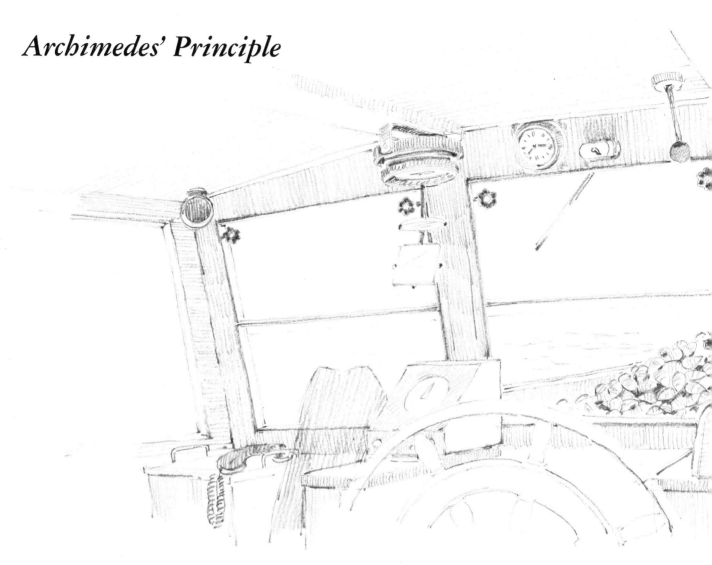

The view from the helm ....

As more and more beets
were dumped into the hold,
the barge sank deeper
into the water.
Soon water lapped right
over the deck!
How could such a heavy boat
still stay afloat, I wondered.
The skipper gave me
a little demonstration
to explain
what is known as
Archimedes' Principle.

He took a pan of water, a tin cup,
and some coins.

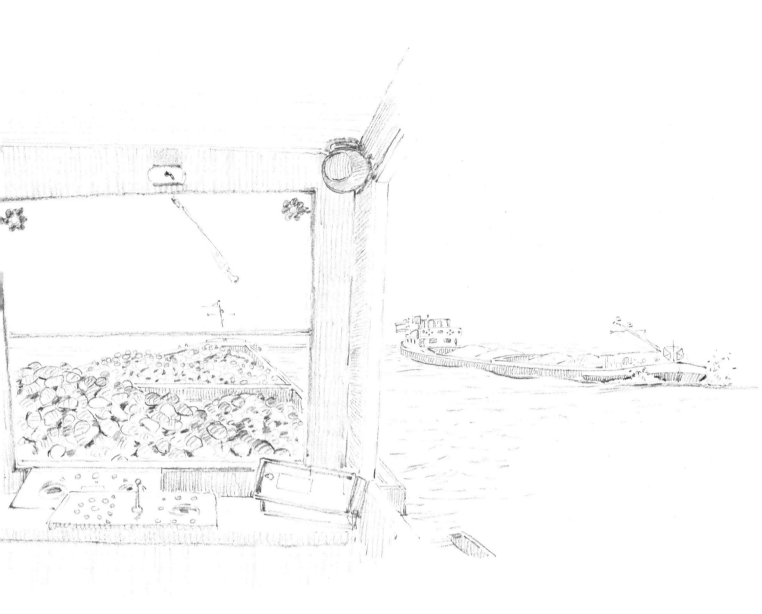

... sugar beets as far as the eye can see!

The empty cup floated high
on the surface. Filling the
cup with coins made it sink a
bit, and at the same time the water
level rose. The weighted cup exerted a force equal to
the weight of the water it *displaced,* and
the water's pressure against the cup kept it afloat.
When the lesson was over...

In Holland, a land made from the sea,
    there is a department of the government
called the Water Ministry.
    The "Waterstaat" looks after dikes,
the drainage of polders, and the depth of
    the waterways. Here is one of its boats
                        on patrol.

. . . we were on our way!

You never stop waving aboard ship!
Passers-by on ship and shore all return a wave
            and a smile.

Navigating

Just like drivers on the road,
skippers need signs
and signals
to guide their ships safely.
Here is a sampling
of the most frequent ones
I saw.

"I'm passing to the right!"

Ships on european waterways pass each other to the left, just like cars do. However, the ship travelling upstream can decide to pass to the right, if necessary. By day, the ship displays a blue shield to convey its intentions, by night, a flashing light.

Keep Right

Forbidden to Anchor

Whistle!

Speed Limit 6 km. per hour.

No Entry

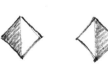

Keep between these markers

No Parking

Red Light

Red buoy

River entry sign, here for the River IJssel, looks just like one on a motorway!

green light

— Channel —

Black buoy with a white light.

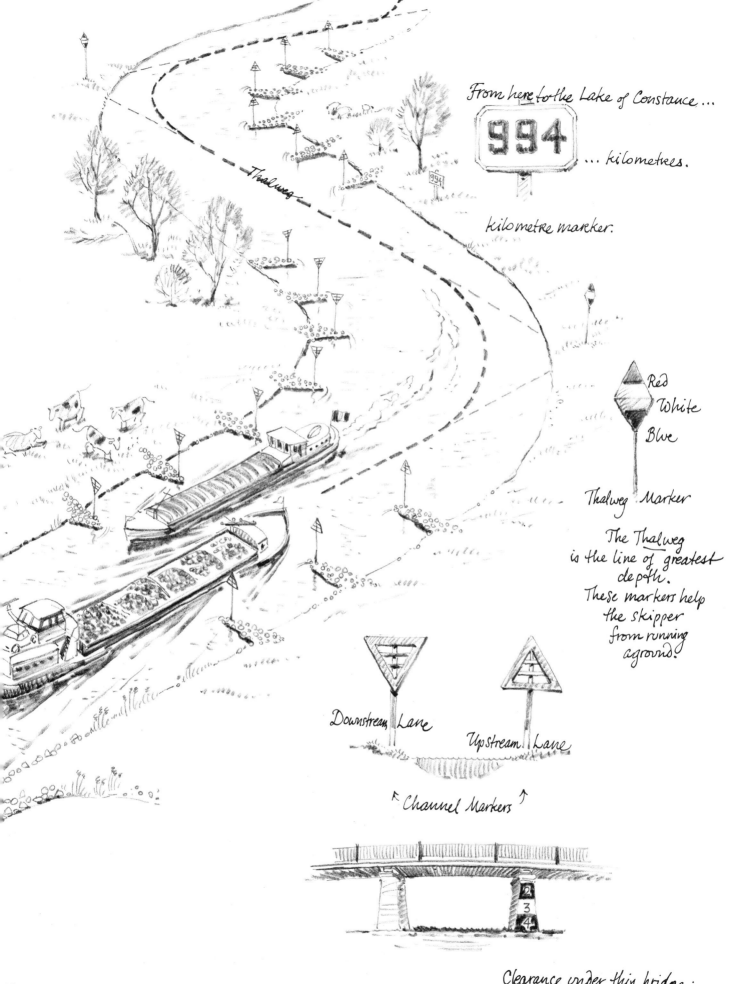

From here to the Lake of Constance...

994

... kilometres.

kilometre marker.

Thalweg

Red
White
Blue

Thalweg Marker

The Thalweg is the line of greatest depth. These markers help the skipper from running aground.

Downstream Lane

Upstream Lane

← Channel Markers →

2
3
4

Clearance under this bridge:
4 Metres.

The Rhine

Heavy traffic on the Rhine, through the Ruhr.

Part of our trip was along the lower Rhine River. I only saw it on the radar, since it was night-time. However, I know it is Europe's most important waterway, linking Rotterdam with the industrial Ruhr region of Germany, as well as French cities like Strasbourg, and even Basel in Switzerland. The Rhine is also well known for the wines that come from its shores.

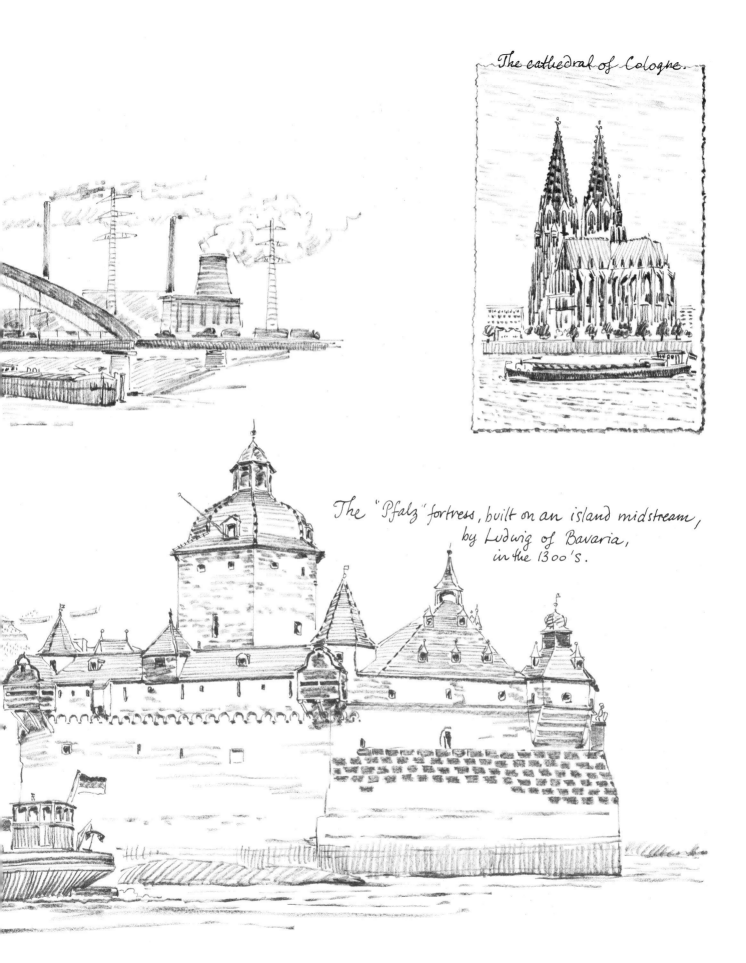

The cathedral of Cologne.

The "Pfalz" fortress, built on an island midstream,
by Ludwig of Bavaria,
in the 1300's.

While her husband snatches
a bite to eat belowstairs,
Mrs. van Wynen takes the wheel.

Sailing by night

When darkness fell, Mr. Van Wynen did
not tie up his ship for the night,
but continued on his way, navigating with the aid of radar.
During the sugar beet harvest, the Van Wynens' ship
works 24 hours a day, husband and wife taking turns
at the helm.
Time is money!

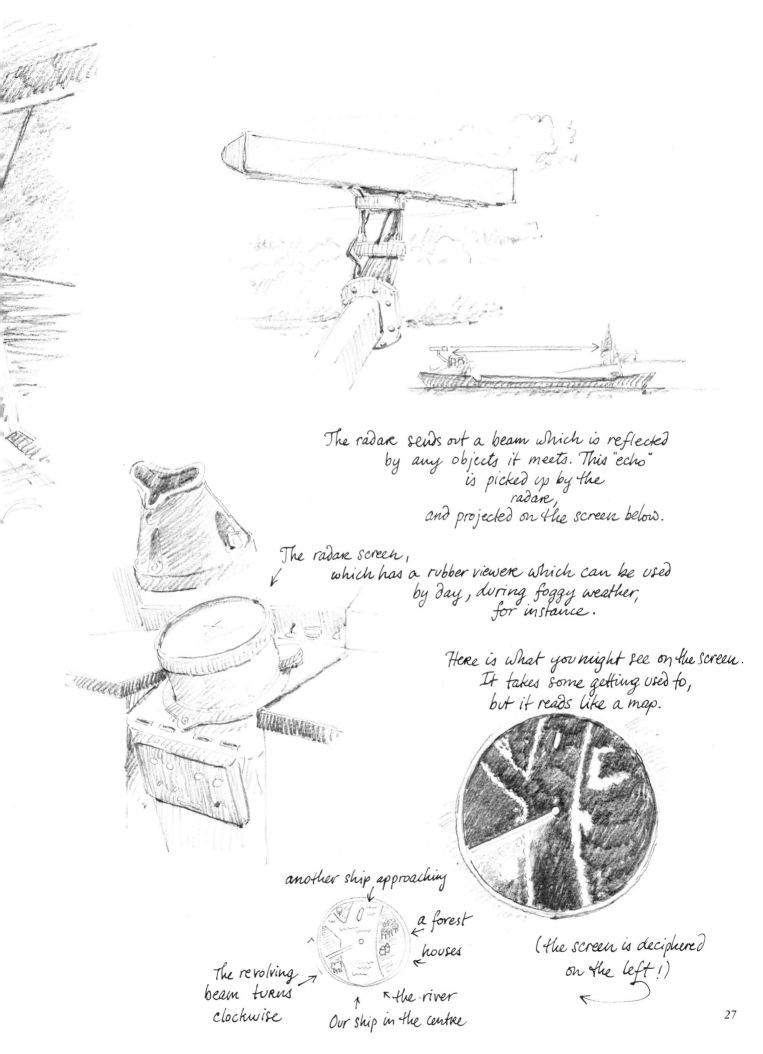

The radar sends out a beam which is reflected
by any objects it meets. This "echo"
is picked up by the
radar,
and projected on the screen below.

The radar screen,
which has a rubber viewer which can be used
by day, during foggy weather,
for instance.

Here is what you might see on the screen.
It takes some getting used to,
but it reads like a map.

another ship approaching

a forest

houses

The revolving
beam turns
clockwise

the river

Our ship in the centre

(the screen is deciphered
on the left!)

Early the next morning,
a small boat came alongside
to refuel the Van Wynens' barge with diesel fuel.
A barge as big as the Van Wynens'
needs a lot of power, and the engine
burns no less than 100 litres (26.5 gallons)
an hour.

The small boat carries everything to keep a
ship happy.
There's oil,
grease,
propane...

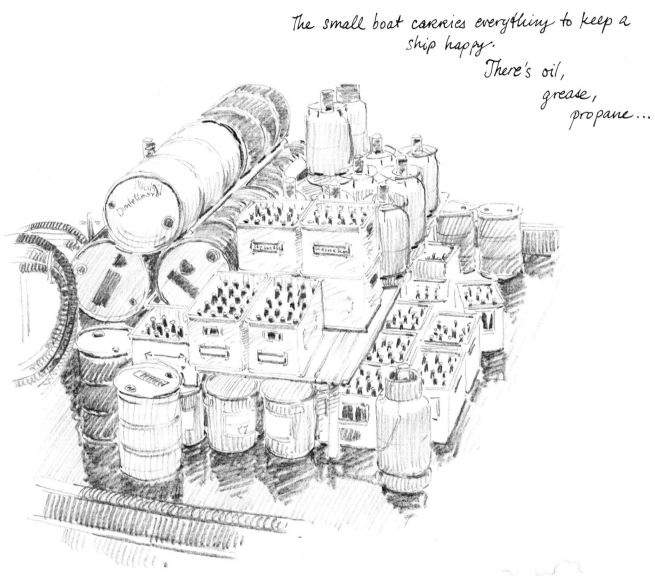

... and even beer
for the captain!

At our destination—the sugar refinery—huge cranes
waited to unload the barge.
Swinging their huge shovels back and
forth, they piled the beets
into mountains by the quay.
What an impressive sight!

Finishing touch

To pick up the last remaining beets in the hold,
a small bulldozer was lowered down by crane.
It artfully shuffled all the random beets
into a neat pile for the shovel.
Then the boat was given a good hosing down—
Mr. Van Wynen likes his house kept tidy!

The weekend

At the end of a busy week,
the Van Wynens need a rest.
They tie up the boat,
and with the aid of the small crane on board,
lower their car to the quay.

Bye! Bye!

In Belgium

Belgium, like Holland,
is a flat land
located near the mouth of the Rhine.
Waterway transport is as important here
as it is in Holland.
To accommodate the big modern barges
that travel the Rhine and the Lowlands,
the Belgians have widened and deepened
many of the major waterways.

The church
of the Holy Virgin in
Antwerp overlooks
the River Schelde,
and one of the world's
busiest seaports.

One of the city gates in Tournus bestrides the river Schelde. (Escaut)

Other canals are just big enough to carry the traditional "Flemish barges" that are still the principal type of barge used in Belgium's neighbour, France. Let's have a look...

In France

Unlike Holland and Belgium,
France is a country of diverse terrain.

The French built a canal system
using locks, so that boats could travel
throughout the country. Most canals in France
preserve the charm of the bygone days
in which they were built.
Indeed, France, unlike her neighbours
on the Rhine, hasn't modernized many
of her canals, and the barges you see
there today are the same ones
your great-grandfather could have seen.

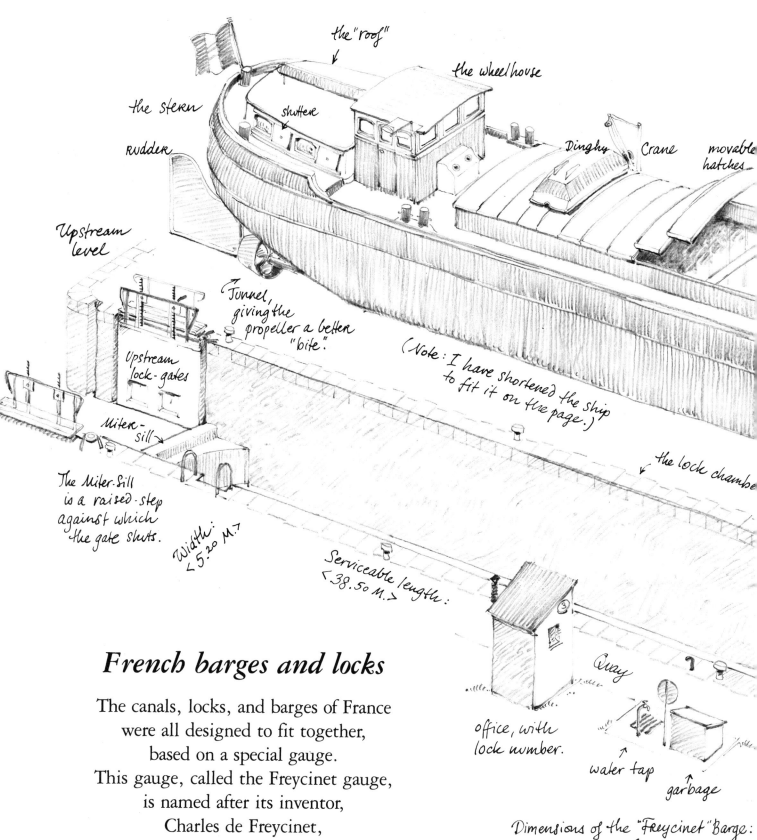

the "roof"

the wheelhouse

the stern

shutter

rudder

Dinghy

Crane

movable hatches

Upstream level

Tunnel, giving the propeller a better "bite."

Upstream lock-gates

(Note: I have shortened the ship to fit it on the page.)

Miter-sill

The Miter-sill is a raised step against which the gate shuts.

the lock chamber

Width: < 5.20 M. >

Serviceable length: < 38.50 M. >

Quay

office, with lock number.

water tap

garbage

French barges and locks

The canals, locks, and barges of France
were all designed to fit together,
based on a special gauge.
This gauge, called the Freycinet gauge,
is named after its inventor,
Charles de Freycinet,
minister of public works in 1878.
This gauge is based on the dimensions
of the Flemish barge,
the most popular of that time.

Dimensions of the "Freycinet" Barge:

Length: 38.50 M.   Draft: 1.80 M.
Width: 5.06 M.   Tonnage: 240 Ton
Volume of the hold: 405 M³.

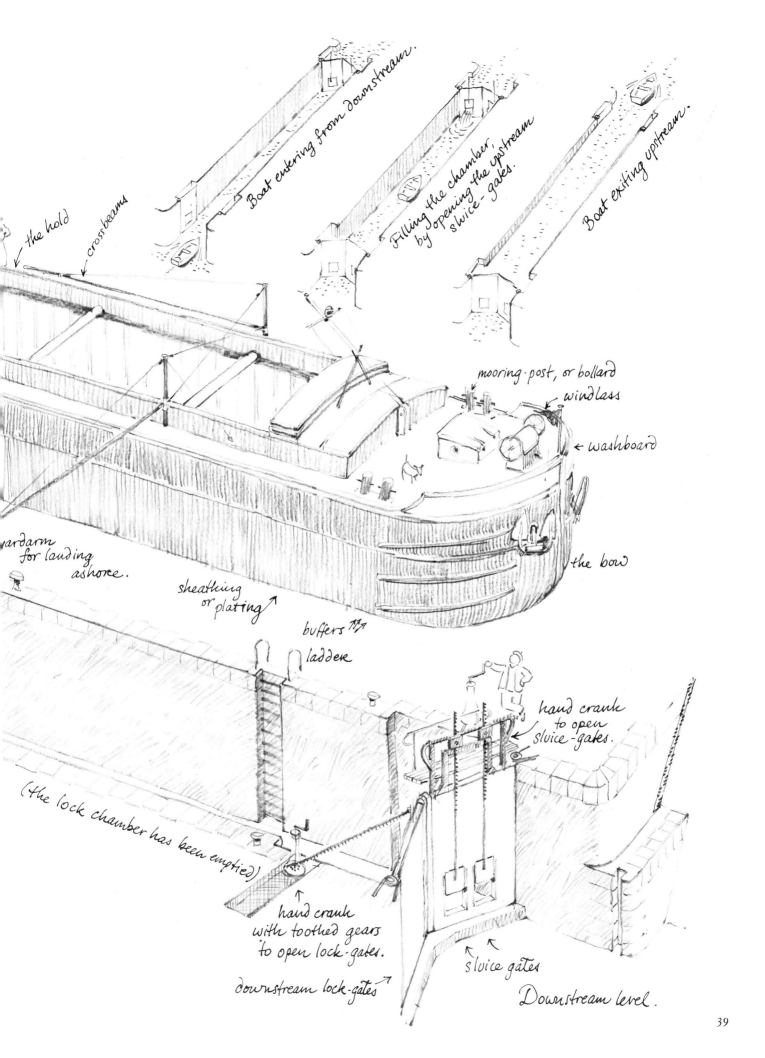

Boat entering from downstream.

Filling the chamber, by opening the upstream sluice-gates.

Boat exiting upstream.

the hold

crossbeams

mooring-post, or bollard

windlass

← washboard

yardarm for landing ashore.

sheathing or plating ↗

the bow

buffers ↗↗↗

ladder

(the lock chamber has been emptied)

hand crank to open sluice-gates.

hand crank with toothed gears to open lock-gates.

downstream lock-gates ↗

sluice gates

Downstream level.

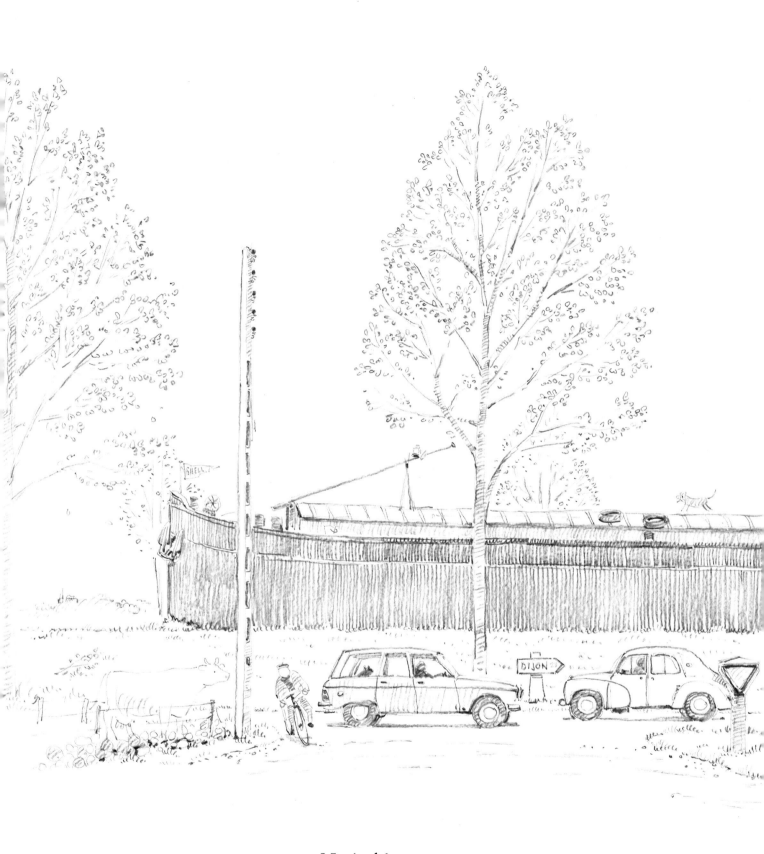

Navigable waterways
criss cross much of the French nation.

And there are surprising sights to be seen
hundreds of miles from the sea.

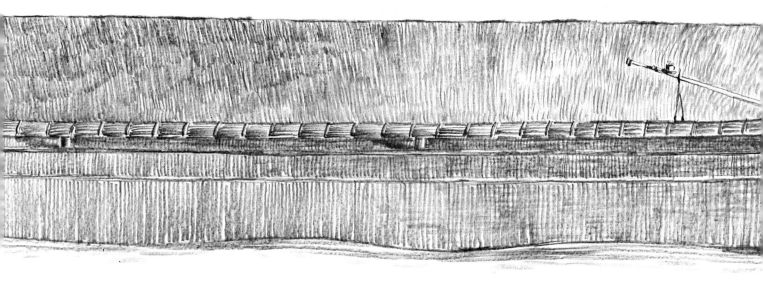

These remarkable canals take ships deep under hill...

An aqueduct on the canal from the
River Marne, to the Rhine.

. . . and high over dale!

Life on board

Bargemen didn't always live aboard ship
with their families. Long ago, they lived on shore,
working their barges locally by day.
But then came the railway, bringing stiff competition
to the bargemen. To keep his customers,
the bargeman had to keep his prices low.
So he dispensed with his house and his crewmen
and brought his family to live on board and help him.

Inside a French barge

Most French barges are much smaller than Mr. Van Wynen's,

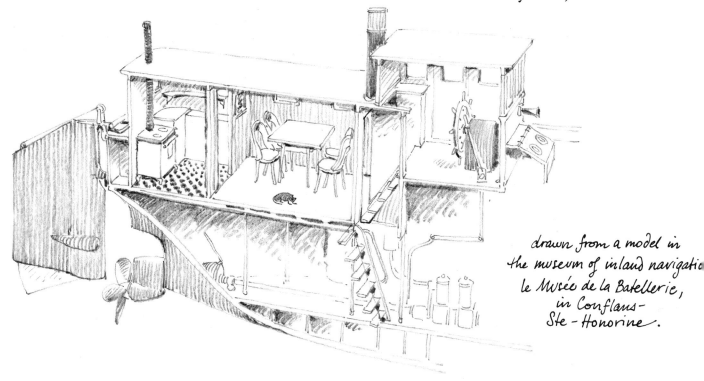

drawn from a model in
the museum of inland navigatio
le Musée de la Batellerie,
in Conflans-
Ste-Honorine.

in order to travel the narrow canals.

In the living room.

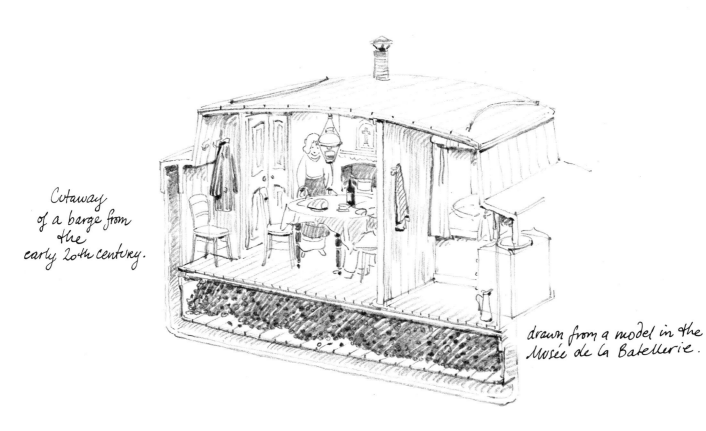

Cutaway
of a barge from
the
early 20th century.

drawn from a model in the
Musée de la Batellerie.

Before barges had their own engines,
they had to be hauled along from the shore
by horses and sometimes men.

There were always
two towpaths,
one on each side of the waterway,
so that ships could
pass without entangling
their towropes.

A pair of tow-horses was called
"une courbe".

In the last century when skippers
brought their families on board to live,
it was impossible for children to
go to school, for they were
always travelling.

Unable to learn other trades, boat-children
knew only what they had learned aboard
ship, and inevitably they became skippers themselves
when they grew up. Mr. Van Wynen, for instance,
is the son of a skipper, of a skipper, of a skipper!
Today, all children must attend elementary school;
for boat-children, it means going
to special boarding school at the age of six.
Children and parents can only get together
on occasional weekends and holidays. Even today,
most boat-children leave school early,
to return to the family barge and help their parents
navigate. A boating son can eventually buy
his father's barge, and the retired captain
and his wife are able to live ashore—
but never too far from the sight of water!

Whoever has owned a boat
knows that the work
is never done.

A boat always needs washing...
repainting...
and numerous odd
repairs below deck
to keep her shipshape!

How the bargeman finds his work

Accompanying each shipment
is a way-bill (*lettre de voiture*).
Once the skipper delivers
a shipment, the recipient signs
the way-bill, with the date and hour.

The Way-Bill

With this document in hand,
the skipper presents himself to the
nearest Labour Exchange
(*La Bourse du Travail*).
Here, based on the
date of his last shipment,
the skipper receives a number
and is invited to attend
the next session of the Exchange.

At the same time, freight brokers
inform the Exchange of
the various shipments to be made.

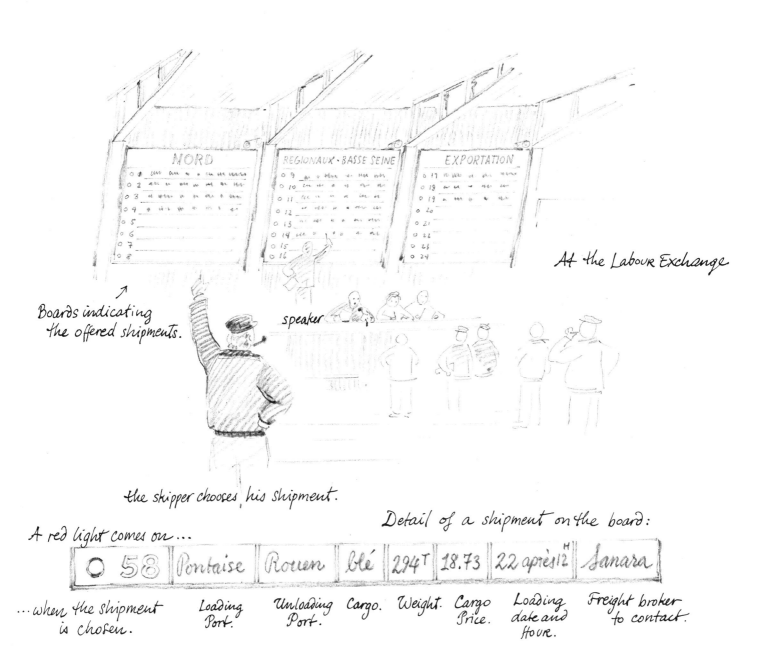

At the Labour Exchange

Boards indicating the offered shipments.

speaker

the skipper chooses his shipment.

A red light comes on...

Detail of a shipment on the board:

| ○ 58 | Pontaise | Rouen | blé | 294ᵀ | 18.73 | 22 après 12ᴴ | Sanara |

...when the shipment is chosen.

Loading Port.

Unloading Port.

Cargo.

Weight.

Cargo Price.

Loading date and Hour.

Freight broker to contact.

Once or twice a week the Exchange has a session.
The shipments offered to the skippers are posted on a board.
The skippers are called out by their numbers.
When his turn comes, a skipper chooses the
shipment he would most like to have.
The chosen shipment is marked by a red light.
Once the session is over, the skippers
contact the freight brokers, settle a contract,
and start off on a new journey.

The clock has just struck noon.
The lock is closed for lunch. Luckily there
is a village nearby. There's just enough time
for mother to fetch some groceries.

The children take out the rubbish
and fill up the water tank.
Meanwhile, the captain
looks out for himself!

Paris and Conflans-Sainte-Honorine

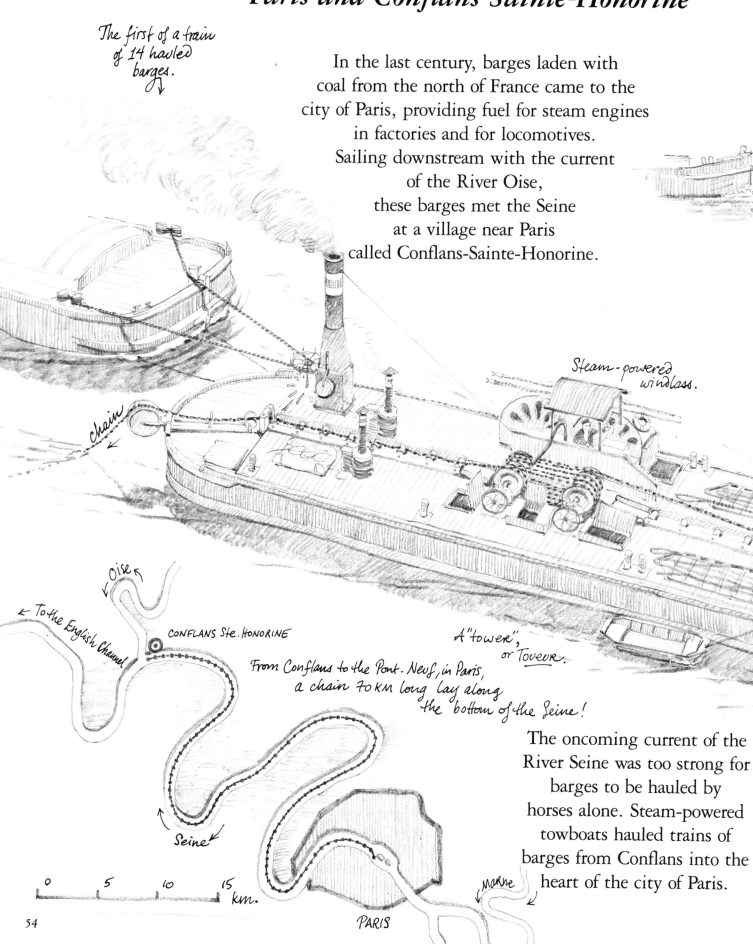

The first of a train of 14 hauled barges.

In the last century, barges laden with coal from the north of France came to the city of Paris, providing fuel for steam engines in factories and for locomotives. Sailing downstream with the current of the River Oise, these barges met the Seine at a village near Paris called Conflans-Sainte-Honorine.

Steam-powered windlass.

chain

Oise

← To the English Channel

CONFLANS Ste. HONORINE

A "tower", or Toueur.

From Conflans to the Pont-Neuf, in Paris, a chain 70 KM long lay along the bottom of the Seine!

Seine

The oncoming current of the River Seine was too strong for barges to be hauled by horses alone. Steam-powered towboats hauled trains of barges from Conflans into the heart of the city of Paris.

0   5   10   15 KM.

Marne

PARIS

The smokestacks could be lowered to pass beneath bridges.

A Tugboat negotiating a bridge.

These towboats had neither paddle wheels nor propellers, but hauled themselves along on a sturdy chain sunk on the riverbed. Although extremely powerful, a towboat was nonetheless limited by the length of its chain. The towboats were gradually replaced by tugboats until barges were provided with engines of their own.

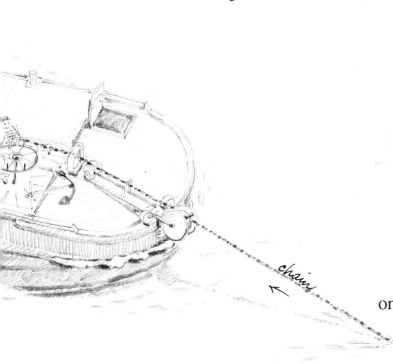

chain

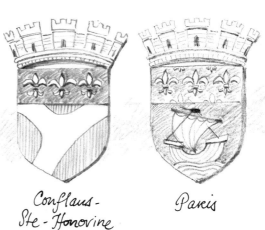

Conflans-Ste-Honorine

Paris

The coats of arms of both cities pay tribute to the River Seine, on whose banks they grew. That of Conflans shows the meeting place of the rivers Seine and Oise. That of Paris shows a ship on the waves, although this city, by water, lies more than 360 kilometres (225 miles) from the sea!

A city of boats . . . Paris!

The old port of Paris

Well before the age of steam,
the waterways of Paris bustled with activity.
Wood, used as a fuel
as well as for building, was floated
downstream to the capital on boats.

In Paris, the wood was dried and
stored on an island in the Seine,
the Ile Louvier, which has since
been joined to the city's right bank.

A French packet-boat, called a "Coche d'Eau

The old port of Paris _from an engraving in the Musée de la Batellerie._

Another flourishing activity in Paris was the arrival
and departure of packet-boats,
or coches d'eau. These boats carried passengers
to and from the capital on the Seine.
Resting overnight in riverside hostelries
along the way, one could travel
through much of France this way.

Ile Louvier in 1736 _from an engraving in the Musée de la Batellerie._

British waterways

The Barton aqueduct, on the Duke of Bridgewater's canal, 1761.

The first canal in Britain was built
by the Duke of Bridgewater in 1761, to transport coal
from his mines to the city of Manchester.
Designed by James Brindley, this canal
even had a tunnel and an aqueduct.
The novel idea made the duke's coal
less expensive and was an immediate success.

Sluice-gate
crank.

The duke's canal inspired a fever of canal building
throughout Britain, linking the major cities.
However, the canal system was short-lived, for the
newly designed railways soon transported goods much faster.

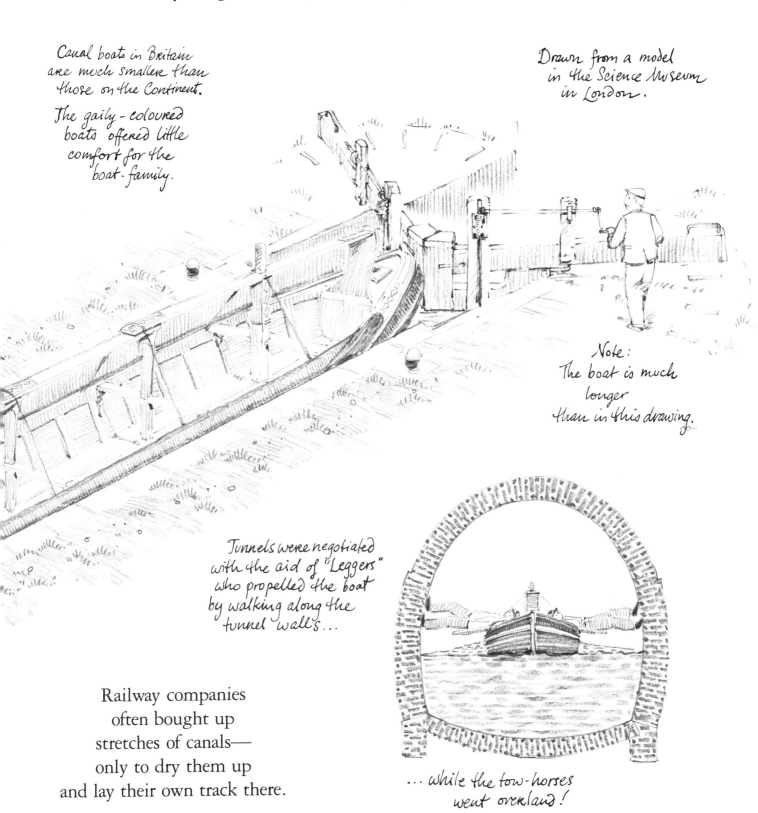

Canal boats in Britain
are much smaller than
those on the Continent.

The gaily-coloured
boats offered little
comfort for the
boat-family.

Drawn from a model
in the Science Museum
in London.

Note:
The boat is much
longer
than in this drawing.

Tunnels were negotiated
with the aid of "Leggers"
who propelled the boat
by walking along the
tunnel walls...

Railway companies
often bought up
stretches of canals—
only to dry them up
and lay their own track there.

...while the tow-horses
went overland!

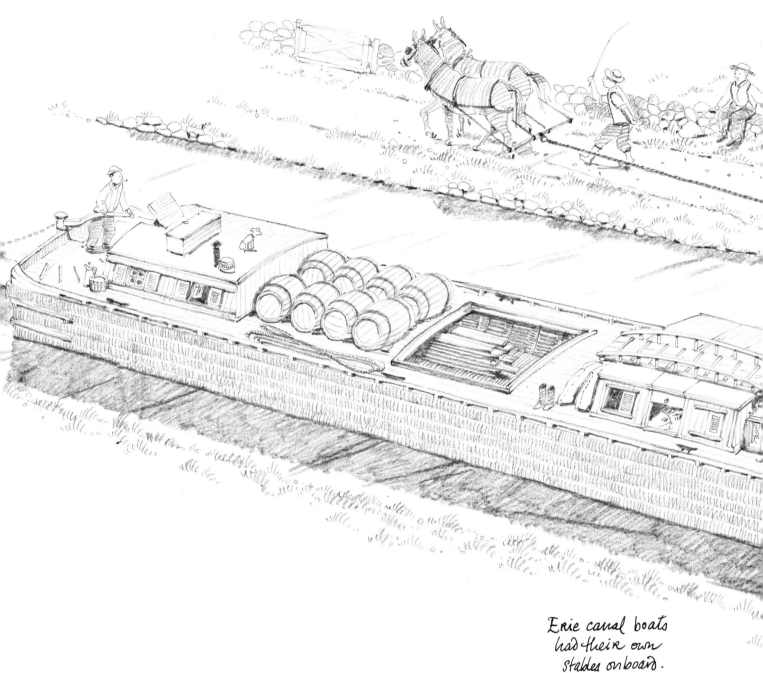

Erie canal boats had their own stables onboard.

The Erie Canal

The first long canal in the United States was the Erie Canal,
opened in 1825. It linked the Hudson River at Albany
with the city of Buffalo on the Great Lakes, thus making
a direct route by water from New York City to the distant
frontiers of the West. The canal allowed profitable transport
in both directions. Manufactured goods from the
East Coast were sent westward to the frontier towns,
and produce and grain came back from the farms, eastward to the
coastal cities. As in England, the canal carried not only freight
but also passengers, aboard comfortable packet-boats.

To pass, the tow-line of
one boat was sunk
beneath the
oncoming ship.

Here, too, the railway made barges obsolete,
and the Erie Canal has been abandoned for years.
However, the United States is rich in large
natural waterways, like the Mississippi.
Here, powerful "pushers," like waterbound locomotives,
convey cargo throughout the centre of the country.
The idea of using pushers spread to Europe, and I was
lucky enough to take a trip through Paris aboard one called the Valois.
Here is what I saw...

The future

A train of barges hauled by a tugboat,
or towboat, needed a crew to steer *each* barge
and keep it in line. However, a train
of *pushed* barges firmly tied together
can be handled as if it were
one long barge.

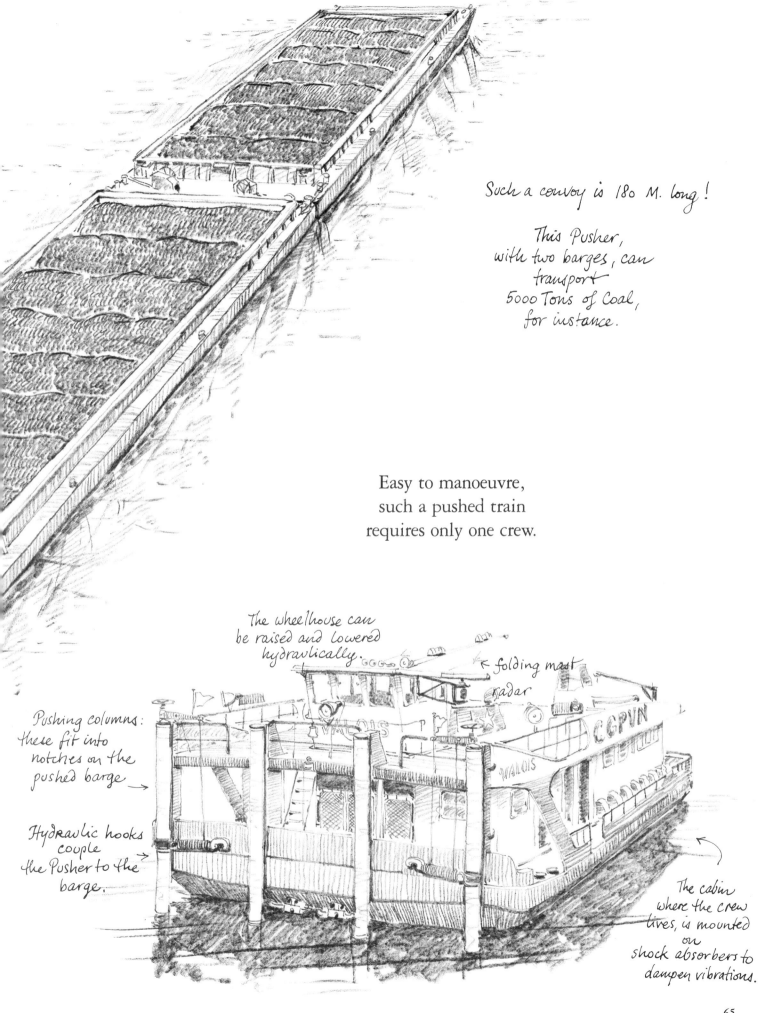

Such a convoy is 180 M. long!

This Pusher, with two barges, can transport 5000 Tons of Coal, for instance.

Easy to manoeuvre,
such a pushed train
requires only one crew.

The wheelhouse can be raised and lowered hydraulically.

← folding mast radar

Pushing columns: these fit into notches on the pushed barge →

Hydraulic hooks couple the Pusher to the barge. →

The cabin where the crew lives, is mounted on shock absorbers to dampen vibrations.

WALOIS

CGPVN

65

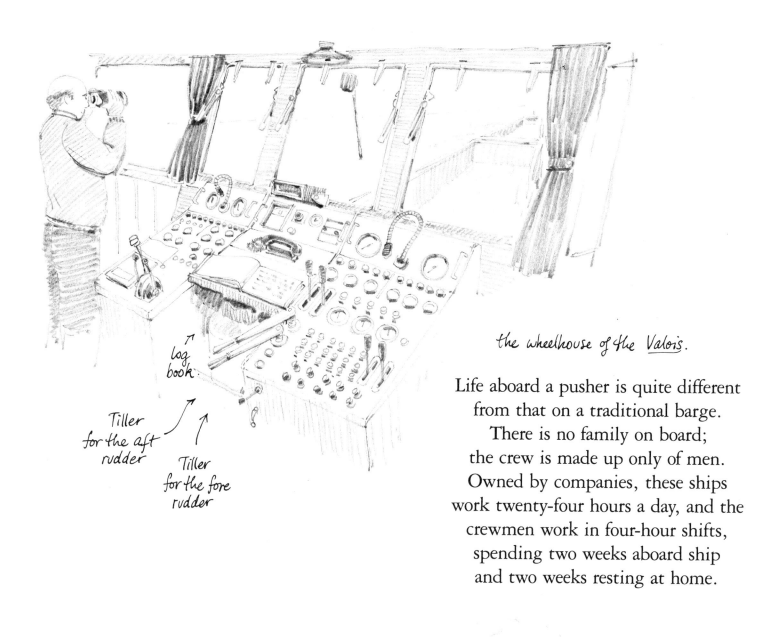

the wheelhouse of the _Valois_.

log
book

Tiller
for the aft
rudder

Tiller
for the fore
rudder

Life aboard a pusher is quite different
from that on a traditional barge.
There is no family on board;
the crew is made up only of men.
Owned by companies, these ships
work twenty-four hours a day, and the
crewmen work in four-hour shifts,
spending two weeks aboard ship
and two weeks resting at home.

Containers

folded mast

SEA MERLAN

EXPRESS

I saw this modern container ship
lying in the very heart of Paris!

The ship you see below is one
I was surprised to see in the centre of Paris.
It is a container ship, able to sail the
high seas but small enough with its telescopic wheelhouse
to pass under bridges and go
through big locks. The containers, stacked
like blocks on board, can be lifted
by crane onto trucks or railway flat waggons.
This versatile system
has a promising future, and is today's
expression of our most
ancient means of transport...

...by waterway!

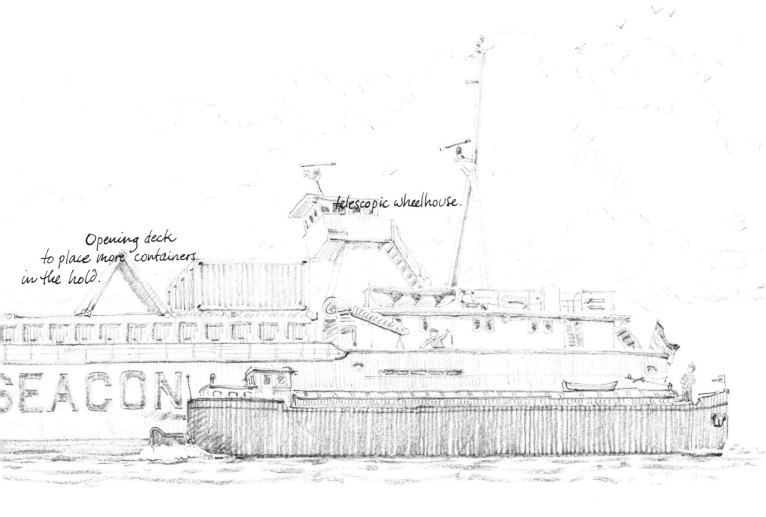

telescopic wheelhouse.

Opening deck
to place more containers
in the hold.

SEACON

Travelling on quiet canals, far from highways
and towns, can take one back to romantic times
when distances were measured in days and not minutes.
Indeed, barges are still allowed to travel at only
6 kilometres (3.5 miles) per hour on many canals, so as not to
destroy the canal banks with their wake!
Nevertheless, this mode of transport—too often forgotten—
is most economical, which should guarantee it an important
place in the future.

My Sources

Le Musée d' Intérêt National de la Batellerie,
Conflans-Sainte-Honorine, (Yvelines), France

The Science Museum, London

Office National de Navigation, Paris

Encyclopedia Britannica

La Batellerie et Conflans-Sainte-Honorine
by François Beaudouin

The Erie Canal
by Peter Spier

Ships
by Björn Landström

Voies d' Eau et Bateliers du Nord,
by the Centre National de Documentation Pédagogique
and the Centre Régional de Documentation Pédagogique de Lille, France

. . . and my thanks

to Mr. and Mrs. Piet Van Wynen,
as well as to Mr. Paul Brinkman,
for my trip on a barge

to Mr. Ludovic de Noue, and to the entire crew of the pusher Valois
of the Compagnie Générale des Pousseurs
sur les voies navigables (CGPVN), in Paris

to Mr. Michel Zeller,
Mr. Charly Godefroy,
and Mr. Martial Chantre.

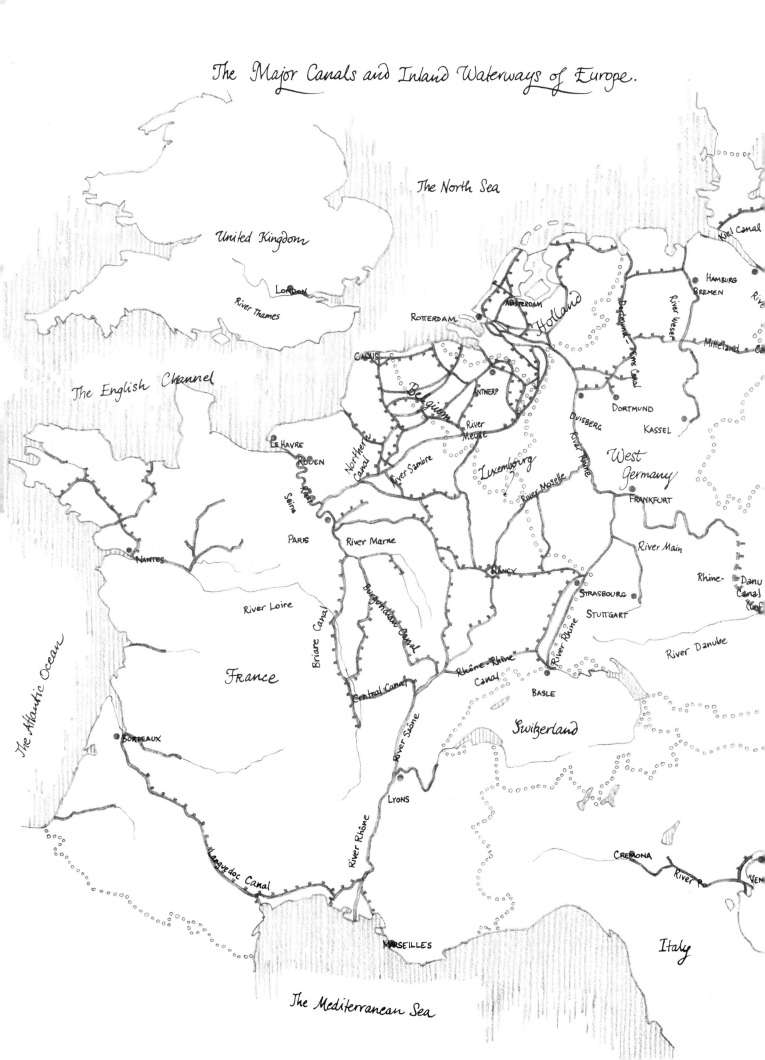

The Major Canals and Inland Waterways of Europe.

The North Sea

United Kingdom

London

River Thames

The English Channel

Kiel Canal

HAMBURG

BREMEN

River Weser

River

AMSTERDAM

Holland

ROTTERDAM

Dortmund-Ems Canal

Mitteland Ca

CALAIS

Belgium

ANTWERP

River Meuse

DUISBERG

DORTMUND

KASSEL

West Germany

Le Havre

ROUEN

Northern Canal

River Sambre

Luxembourg

River Moselle

River Rhine

FRANKFURT

Seine

PARIS

River Marne

NANCY

River Main

Rhine-
Danu
Canal
Cua

STRASBOURG

STUTTGART

River Loire

Briare Canal

Burgundian Canal

River Rhine

River Danube

France

Central Canal

Rhône-Rhine Canal

BASLE

Switzerland

The Atlantic Ocean

BORDEAUX

River Saône

LYONS

CREMONA

River P

VEN

Languedoc Canal

River Rhône

MARSEILLES

Italy

The Mediterranean Sea